W9-CAJ-729

Germs

Written by Judy Oetting
Illustrated by Tad Herr

Children's Press®
A Division of Scholastic Inc.
New York • Toronto • London • Auckland • Sydney
Mexico City • New Delhi • Hong Kong
Danbury, Connecticut

Dear Parents/Educators,

Welcome to Rookie Ready to Learn. Each Rookie Reader in this series includes additional age-appropriate Let's Learn Together activity pages that help your young child to be better prepared when starting school. *Germs* offers opportunities for you and your child to talk about the important social/emotional skill of **how our actions affect others**. Here are early-learning skills you and your child will encounter in the *Germs* Let's Learn Together pages:

• Rhyming
• Patterns
• Counting

We hope you enjoy sharing this delightful, enhanced reading experience with your early learner.

Library of Congress Cataloging-in-Publication Data

Oetting, Judy.
  Germs/written by Judy Oetting; illustrated by Tad Herr.
    p. cm. — (Rookie ready to Learn)
  ISBN 978-0-531-26500-0 — ISBN 978-0-531-26732-5 (pbk.)
  1. Bacteria—Juvenile literature.
  I. Herr, Tad, 1955– ill. II. Title. III. Series.

  QR57.O35 2011
  616.9'201—dc22

                          2010049912

3 4 5 6 7 8 9 10 R 18 17 16 15 14 13

Wash your hands!
Scrub them clean!

Tiny germs cannot be seen.

They hide.
They creep
beneath the nails.

They have eyes,
feet, and tails.

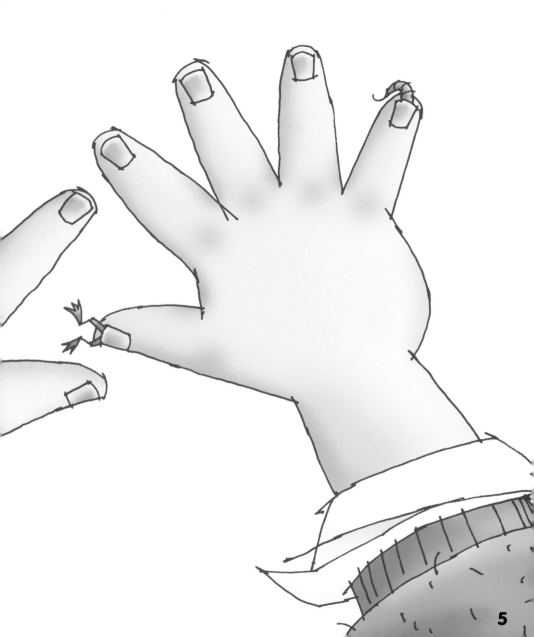

Beware! They're there!

Lick your fingers.
Chew your nails.

Germs in your mouth
will never fail.

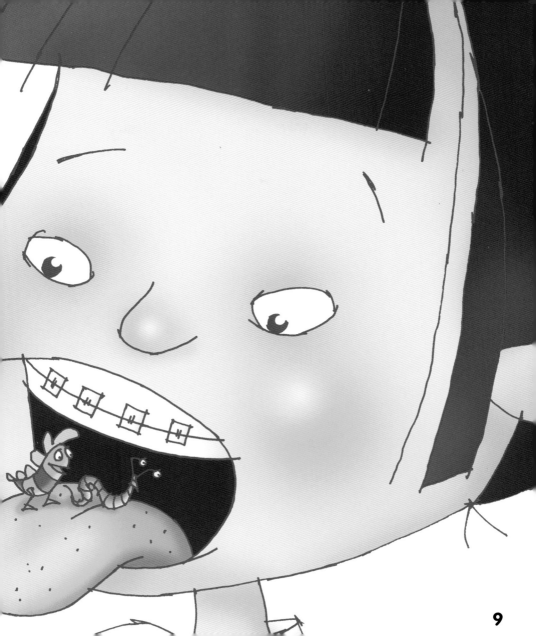

Down the tummy they will go.

They'll have lots of fun below.

Cover your mouth
before you sneeze.

Germs travel fast
to spread disease.

Faster than
cheetahs or
speeding cars!

Run away!
Go very far!

Beware! They're there!

19

Wash hands!
Scrub them!
Keep them clean.

Germs are bad.
Germs are mean.

20

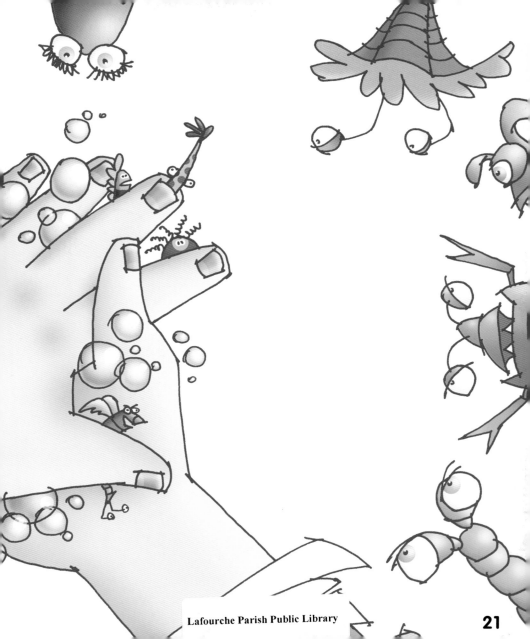

Yucky germs
cannot be seen.

Wash fingers
in between.

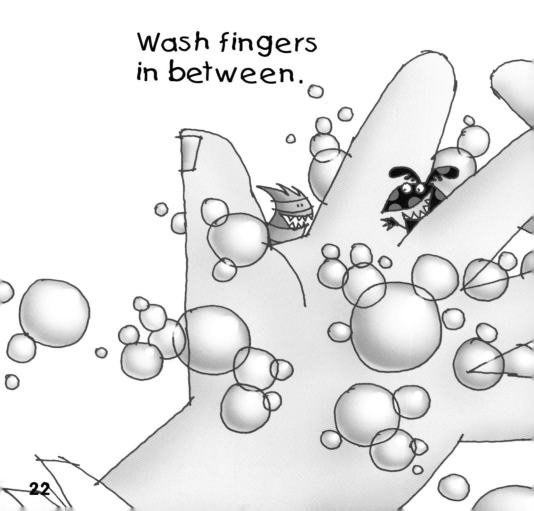

22

Beware! They're there!

Wash your hands.
Don't spread disease.

Wash them often.
Use soap, please!

It's important that you do.

Don't forget! Dry them, too!

Germs are everywhere!

Congratulations!

You just finished reading *Germs* and learned about how to be a healthier you.

About the Author
Judy Oetting taught school for 33 years. She loves writing children's books, and presents programs in science and nature for schools and libraries.

About the Illustrator
Tad Herr has been an illustrator and graphic designer for more than 35 years.

Rookie READY TO LEARN
ACTIVITY BOOK
Germs
Let's learn together!

Wash, Wash, Wash Your Hands

(Sing this song to the tune of "Row, Row, Row Your Boat.")

Wash, wash, wash your hands.
Scrub them nice and clean.
To keep away those little germs
Too tiny to be seen!

Wash, wash, wash your hands
And fingers in between.
Use some soap and water, too.
That will keep them clean!

PARENT TIP: Draw your child's attention to the second hand on a clock. Help your child count the ticks for 15 to 20 seconds — the amount of time it should take for washing hands. That is about the amount of time it takes to sing this song.

Germs Are Everywhere

There are all different kinds of germs in this book. These germs are making patterns. Look at each row. Then point to the germ that comes next.

1.

2.

3.

PARENT TIP: Identifying and exploring patterns helps build math skills. As children learn to recognize visual patterns, they are able to make predictions about their observations and guess what comes next in a sequence.

35

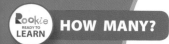

Hidden Germs!

Can you find the hidden germs

on the girl's hands? Have fun counting the germs before she washes them away!

- Count how many germs are hiding on one hand.
- Count how many germs are hiding on the other hand.
- Count how many germs are hiding on both hands.
- Point to the hand where the most germs are hiding.

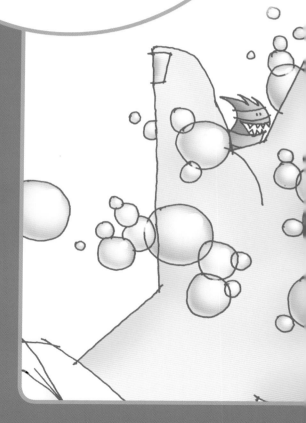

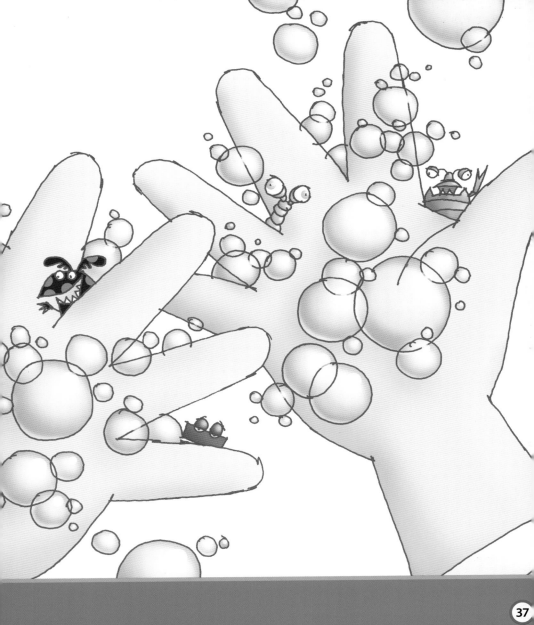

Germs Travel Fast!

The girl in the book washes her hands to keep germs away. Read the rhyme about germs below. Fill in the blanks with your own words.

Tiny germs are all around.

They hide in my _____ and at the playground.
                        name of place

Germs are _____ and _____, I say!
            describing word   describing word

That's why it is important to keep them away!

PARENT TIP: Discuss with your child how washing our hands helps keep us from getting sick. Talk about when we should wash our hands — before eating or after touching pets, playing outside, using the bathroom, or visiting someone who is sick.

I'm a Germ Stopper!

The girl in the book learned to keep germs away. Now it's your turn. Make a germ-stopper badge!

YOU WILL NEED: Construction paper

Markers **Scissors**

1
With a grown-up's help, draw the shape of a stop sign on the paper. Write your name in the middle.

2
Then write one way you can stop germs. Cut out your badge. Have fun wearing your germ-stopper badge.

Germs Word List (79 Words)

and	down	keep	that
are	dry	lick	the
away	everywhere	lots	them
bad	eyes	mean	there
be	fail	mouth	they
before	far	nails	they'll
below	fast	never	they're
beneath	faster	of	tiny
between	feet	often	to
beware	fingers	or	too
cannot	forget	please	travel
cars	fun	run	tummy
cheetahs	germs	scrub	use
chew	go	seen	very
clean	hands	sneeze	wash
cover	have	soap	will
creep	hide	speeding	you
disease	important	spread	your
do	in	tails	yucky
don't	it's	than	

PARENT TIP: With your child, look through the list and see how many names for people's body parts you can find. Hint: There are seven of them! Write down the words and discuss with your child ways we can keep those body parts healthy!